JULIE VERHOEVEN
CONTENTS

SHORT HISTORY
REPRESENTATIVE
IMAGE
PROJECT

Q&A

JULIE VERHOEVEN SHORT HISTORY

ジュリー・ヴァーホーヴェンの作品とキャリアは非常に多様でそれぞれの作品が今までの歩みを定義している。彼女は主にファッションの世界に関わってきたものの、その世界に限定してしまうのは彼女について十分に説明することにはならないだろう。一見すると、世界トップクラスのファッションブランドやGIBOにおける仕事でかなりの注目を集めているが、彼女の作品はアートの世界でもかなり高く評価されている。彼女のスタイルやインスピレーションはもはや作品という枠を超えて現代社会、過去、未来を表現しているといえる。

ジュリーは1969年、イギリスのケント州で非常にクリエイティブな家庭に生まれた。グラフィックデザイナーである父とイラストレーターの母に多大な影響を受け現在の職を選んだといえる。16歳で高校を卒業しMedway College of Art and Designにてファッションの資格を取

得するコースを受けた。おしゃれをすることや洋服全般が大好きだったジュリーは、まだ大学のコースを取るには年齢が達していなかったためこの準備コースを取るのが妥当な選択であった。コースの内容は幅広く、パターンカッティング、裁縫、イラストレーションなどが組み込まれていた。その後St Martinsに入学する気だったが受け入れられなかったため、ジョン・ガリアーノのアシスタントとして働くことを決意。その間も再度St Martinsを受けてみたが不合格であった。それから4年間はガリアーノのデザインアシスタントとしてデザインリサーチ、プリントデザイン、イラストレーションなどを担当し勤めた。ガリアーノの元で働いたことにより多くを学び、その後の彼女のキャリアに繋がる基盤を築きあげることができたといえる。

この頃になってジュリーはイラストレーションの道をさ

らに追求したいと思うようになっていた。ただ彼女の仕事はファッション関係が主であったためなかなかイラストレーションの仕事には恵まれなかった。この頃同時にイラストレーションを指導しはじめてもいた。

いくつかの機会に恵まれパリにてマルティーヌ・シットボンのコレクションデザインを受け持つことになり、再びファッション業界で活躍することになった。テキスタイルのデザインからアクセサリーまで幅広く担当した。1995年にはロンドンに戻りマルティーヌ・シットボンの仕事をフリーランスとして続けつつ、ファッションやイラストレーションの仕事も増やしていった。また学士と修士課程の講議を受け持つことによりさらに仕事は増えていった。

本書では彼女のその後のキャリアがいかに発展していったかを作品を見ながら知ることができる。

The work and career of Julie Verhoeven is an incredibly diverse and image defining history. Whilst her work is settled in the world of fashion this would be a too restrictive definition. On the surface her work is seen in some of the most prestigious fashion titles in the world and her work for Gibo garners many column inches. She is also well represented and exhibited within the art world. Bearing all of this in mind her style and influence has transcended the work itself and has become woven into the fabric of image and identity of the modern world describing the present, referencing the past and looking to the future all at the same time.

Julie was born in Kent, England, in 1969, into a very creative household. Julie regards the encouragement of a graphic designer father and an illustrator mother as being a highly important key to motivating her in her chosen career. This environment is seen as nurturing her desire to pursue a creative path but it was grounded

in her parents' influence in being realistic in what could be achieved. Julie left school at 16 and enrolled at Medway College of Art and Design on a Fashion Diploma course. She had always loved dressing up and clothes in general and, as she was too young for a foundation course, this seemed to be the most appropriate path for her to take. The course itself was quite loose covering pattern cutting and sewing but also illustration. Julie then applied for the degree course at Saint Martins, in London, but was not accepted. She chose instead to work for John Galliano, as a placement, applying again but with no luck. At this point she became a design assistant and continued to work for him for the next four years conducting design research, print design and illustration amongst other activities. Working for Galliano is seen as being the place where a great deal was learnt which has stood her in good stead in her future projects and work.

It was at this point that Julie decided that illustration was something she would like to pursue further. It was regrettable, however, that there was not a lot of commissions available to her coupled with the fact that her work was too fashion oriented. She had also begun to teach the subject.

With the lack of commissions Julie again pursued her fashion career by moving to Paris and working for Martine Sitbon becoming more involved in the design of the collections from textile prints to accessories. In 1995 she returned to London, continuing to work for Martine Sitbon in a freelance capacity, and pursuing numerous freelance commissions along with illustration projects. This was further augmented with lecturing commitments at BA and MA level.

Her career trajectory has taken on a sharper focus with the subsequent pages of this book providing an insight into her work and style.

REPRESENTATIVE IMAGE

2003年1月に行われたモバイルホームギャラリーでの個展、UNFORGIVINGのために作った招待状はジュリーが自分の作品をどのように捉えていたかを表すものでもあり、観客が彼女の作品をどのように受け止めたかを見ることができるジュリーにとって興味深いものであった。招待状には彼女が個展のために作った最初の作品が使用された。カード自体はBARNBROOK DESIGNによってデザインされた。この作品は特に参考にしたものや計画などなく描かれたが次第にキャンバス上に様々な絵が描かれていくうちにルースなりにもスタイルが形成されていった。狙いがわからないような作品にしたいという本人のフィーリングによりさらにルースなスタイルが強調された。この個展を行うことによりファッションではなくアート系の客層を新たに獲得し、彼女の作品に対する新しい認識も得ることができた。

The invitation for her show, Unforgiving, at the Mobile Home gallery in January 2003, is regarded by Julie as a thrilling moment for how she viewed her work and also for an insight into how other people perceived her ideas. The image is taken from the first panel she produced for this exhibition. The invitation itself was designed by Barnbrook Design who returned a finished artwork with the text integrated. This particular panel for the show was approached without any prior knowledge or reference as to how it would turn out but as the panel was filled with images so Julie found a new looseness to her work. This was accompanied by the feeling of not trying to prove any sense of an academic provenance. It also drew a new audience and viewpoint to her work that was more art based and less about the fashion world.

UNFORGIVING / Exhibition Invitation   2003   Mobile Home Gallery, London
Title: Collar and cuffs
Mixed Media on gesso MDF panel
Photography: Jonnie Bassett
Design: Barnbrook Design

Unforgiving

24th January – 9th March 2003

PROJECT 01 SOFT PORN

これはポルノグラフィーではなく、人間の体、特に性器の面白さに魅了され、それを描いた作品で意味深げな性的な絵が重層になって描かれている。ジュリーの作品にとって難点だったのは、彼女の描くものは人間の本性やあまり人に見られることのない人間の行為などをモチーフにしていることだった。そのためポルノというテーマに関連した仕事を受けた時に初めて拘束なく思うがままの作品作りができるようになった。これら作品においてポルノにまつわるネガティブな要素を取り除き象徴性を持たせようとするのが彼女の狙いであった。ポルノの絵を描くことはわいせつな感情からリラックスしたものへと変化していった。彼女の作品が見られれば見られる程、社会の意識は開拓されていったといえる。

It is not pornography, as such, that forms the basis of any interest in the subject but a fascination with the comical aspects of the human form, genitalia in particular. Images of a pornographic nature are loaded with significance and are used in ways that are multi-layered. The crux of Julies work is about human nature and behaviour derived from observation with images being found in places other than the most obvious. It was only when she started to receive commissions that were porn related that her imagination could be given free rein. Julie attempts to get over the negative undertones it is saddled with and introduces symbolism into the subject. It is interesting to point out that illustration did form a very large part of porn magazine content that has lapsed over the last twenty years. The transition into drawing this subject has been a bizarre journey from feeling smutty to being more relaxed with what is being illustrated. It is true to say that the more of this work was seen the more it appeared that Julie had tapped into a stream of public consciousness which has now gathered its own momentum.

Fantasmes par Julie Verhoeven

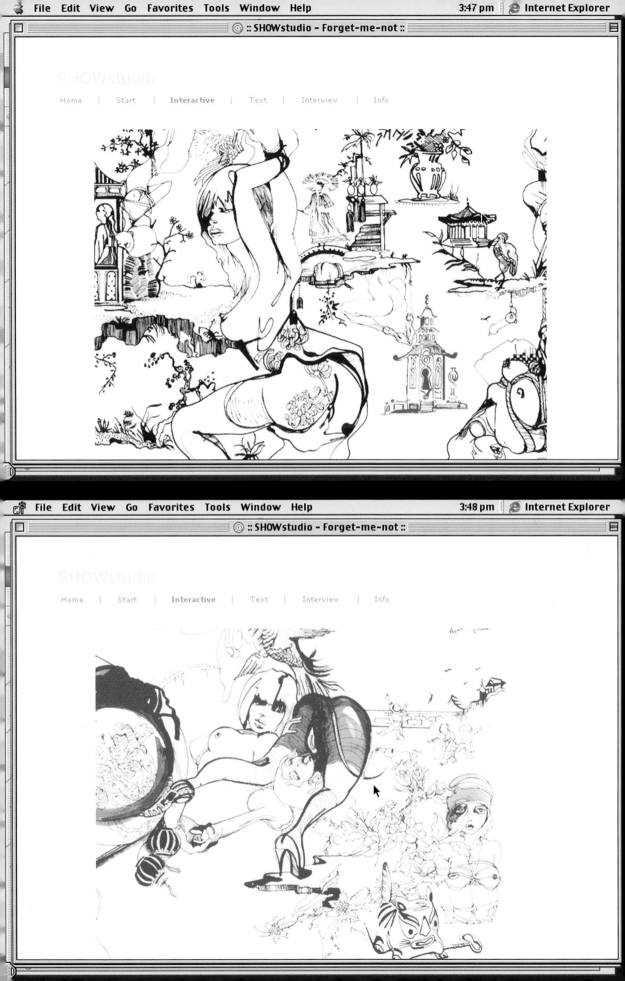

PROJECT 02 GIBO

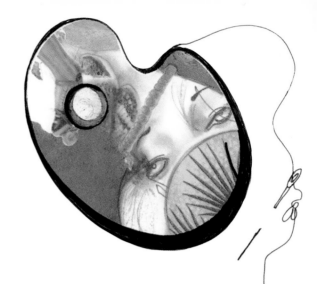

GIBO London
47 CONDUIT STREET, LONDON W1S 2YP
T. 020 7734 2340 F. 020 7734 2344
E. gibo@btconnect.com

GIBO Milan
VIA S. ANDREA. 10/A 20121 MILANO
T. +39 02 799988

Boutique ONWARD
(available GIBO collection)
147, BD ST. GERMAIN PARIS 6e
T. +33 (0)1 55 42 77 55

GIBOはイタリアの洋服製造会社で数々のトップレベルのファッションブランドのためにハイクオリティーな洋服を製造していることで知られる会社である。現在では革新的なデザイナー達のために集中して洋服の製造をしている。しかし会社の社長であるフランコ・ペネはオリジナルのブランド名のもと洋服作りを展開し、クオリティからクリエイティビティまでのコントロールを持ちたいと強く思っていた。マルティーヌ・シットボン時代の同僚であり、GIBOで現在働くベッティナ・オルデンバーグの推薦によりジュリーがデザイナーとしての有力候補にあがった。

個性のあるプリントやカラーを中心にブランド独自のスタイルを確立させることが重要視された。GIBOの洋服を着こなせるような女性像はジュリーが描く女性以外には見当たらなかった。その女性がどのような女性であれ複雑なキャラクターであったことは明白であった。全てのアイデアは直感に頼り発展されていきながらも、一回きりのものではなく、毎回コレクションがあるたびにアクセサリーやショップインテリアなどが増やされブランドが展開されていった。

CHERIE YEOによるショップのインテリアはジュリーのエキシビションとインスタレーションに共鳴し他のショップにはないような統一された世界感を作り出している。またコレクションのステージデザインも同じく重要で、ショーのサウンドトラックはファビオ・アルメイダとエードリアン・セルフによって作られている。

Gibo are an Italian manufacturing company principally known for their high quality production work for a wide number of globally renowned fashion houses. Their focus has become centred on the more uncompromising and challenging designers operating today. However Franco Pené, the president, was very keen to galvanise their own brand name by creating their own line. This would give them ultimate control over quality and also a greater hand in the creative side of the ranges. Bettina Oldenberg, who works for Gibo, and a former colleague from their work at Martine Sitbon, recommended her as being the ideal candidate in realising these ambitions.

From the outset the brand had to have its own discernible identity with an emphasis on print and colour being key components to the designs. There was no obvious Gibo woman in mind with only Julie's characters to draw from. Whatever she appears to be, or can be, she is certainly perceived as being very complex. The ideas are very much a gut reaction and whatever is felt is right. The project has never been regarded as a passing process and, as each collection is created, so more is added from accessories to shop interiors.

The shop architecture and interiors, designed by Cherie Yeo, hark back to Julie's exhibition and installation work and create more of a total world that other labels don't have. The stage design is also important along with the show soundtrack that Fabio Almeida and Adrian Self creates.

AN ASSORTMENT OF SHOW LOOKS FROM GIBO

SPRING / SUMMER 2003
AUTUMN / WINTER 2004

'STEPPING OUT'
'IF LOOKS COULD KILL'

1.

1. <u>WALL DETAIL OF GIBO BOUTIQUE</u> / Conduit Street, London   2003   Photography: Lostrobot

2. <u>ASSORTED DESIGN DRAWINGS FROM GIBO</u>

SPRING / SUMMER 2003   'STEPPING OUT'
AUTUMN / WINTER 2004   'IF LOOKS COULD KILL'
SPRING / SUMMER 2004   'LIFT UP YOUR SKIRT AND FLY'

2.

1.

2.

3.

4.

1.	BARDOT / T-shirt print	Gibo Spring / Summer 2004
2.	PHANTOM / T-shirt print	Gibo Spring / Summer 2004
3.	FLYAWAY BRA / Print	Gibo Spring / Summer 2004
4.	SMOKING NOVICE / Print	Gibo Spring / Summer 2004
5.	PANDORA / Print	Gibo Spring / Summer 2004

1.

2.

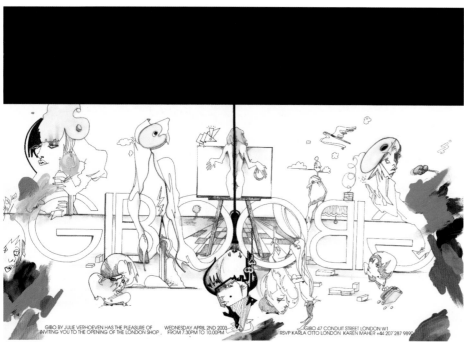

4.

3.

5.

1. <u>GIBO BOUTIQUE LONDON</u> / 'Stepping out'   Photography: Lostrobot
                                                                                        Display: Shona Heath

2. <u>GIBO BOUTIQUE LONDON</u> / Window display detail   Spring / Summer 2003   Photography: Fabio Almeida

3. <u>GIBO BOUTIQUE LONDON</u> / Opening party invitation   April 2003

4. <u>GIBO BOUTIQUE LONDON</u> / Detail of opening window display   2003   Photography: Richard Davies
                                                                                        Display: Shona Heath

5. <u>GIBO BOUTIQUE LONDON</u> / Interior detail   2003   Photography: Richard Davies

6. <u>GIBO BOUTIQUE LONDON</u> / Wall detail   2003   Photography: Jonnie Bassett

7. <u>GIBO BOUTIQUE LONDON</u> / Interior detail   2003   Photography: Emily Burns
                                                                                        Display: Shona Heath

6.

7.

PROJECT 03 EXHIBITIONS

これはジュリーの2回目の個展で、移転した後のモバイルホームギャラリーで行われた。彼女の冷めたムードが反映された作品で前回のポジティブで外交的な雰囲気とは一変した個展となった。ギャラリーのディレクター、ロニー・シンプソンのアイデアでジュリーは1平方メートルの石こうキャンバスに作品を作ることになった。ジュリーは展示会の構成にそれほどこだわりたくはなかったため、それぞれのキャンバスはランダムに作成されつつも、キャンバスの構成は2組、4組、6組ごとに展示されるように決められた。12枚のキャンバスは彼女のスタジオに並べられ、彼女の良いと思うままに壁にかけられた。幻想的なものや性的なものなど様々な絵が重ねられていった。また締めきりがあったため緊張感も加えられ楽しく作業が進められていった。キャンバスでの作業はかなりの長期間をかけて行われたが最終的に全てがまとまったのはクリスマス時期の2週間であった。作品のテーマは人間の影の部分でどちらかというと醜いものが好んで描かれた。モチーフは動物がたくさん描かれ本能と反社会的行動を表している。また面白おかしくではあるが死についても言及している。石こうの滑らかなキャンバスは紙よりも思うがままに絵を描くことをジュリーに可能にさせたようにみえる。

This was Julie's second solo show at the now relocated Mobile Home gallery. Julie's sombre mood was reflected in the work and delivered an opposite feeling from the more outwardly optimistic previous exhibition. Ronnie Simpson, the gallery director, had the idea to give Julie the opportunity to work on one metre square gessoed panels. It was decided to work randomly on each panel with the option of placing them together in groups of two, four or six, though Julie did not want to be too concerned as to how these were to be composed. The twelve panels were all laid out in her studio with them being rotated from floor to wall as she saw fit thus creating a layers to the finished work. There was a provocative layer followed by a layer of fantastical creatures, freeing up the balance to be brasher with. There was an added dynamic of schedule to work within which was both enjoyable and pressured. All panels were worked on over a fairly long time period but it was only in a two-week period at Christmas when everything came together. The themes were about the darker side of human nature with a desire to draw less pretty things. The panels contained lots of animals referencing their primal instincts and the anti-social aspects of their behaviour. They also dealt with death but in a comical way. The gesso surface was felt to allow Julie to move away from paper, its smooth surface allowing her mind to meander - drawing for pleasure without any consequences.

1.

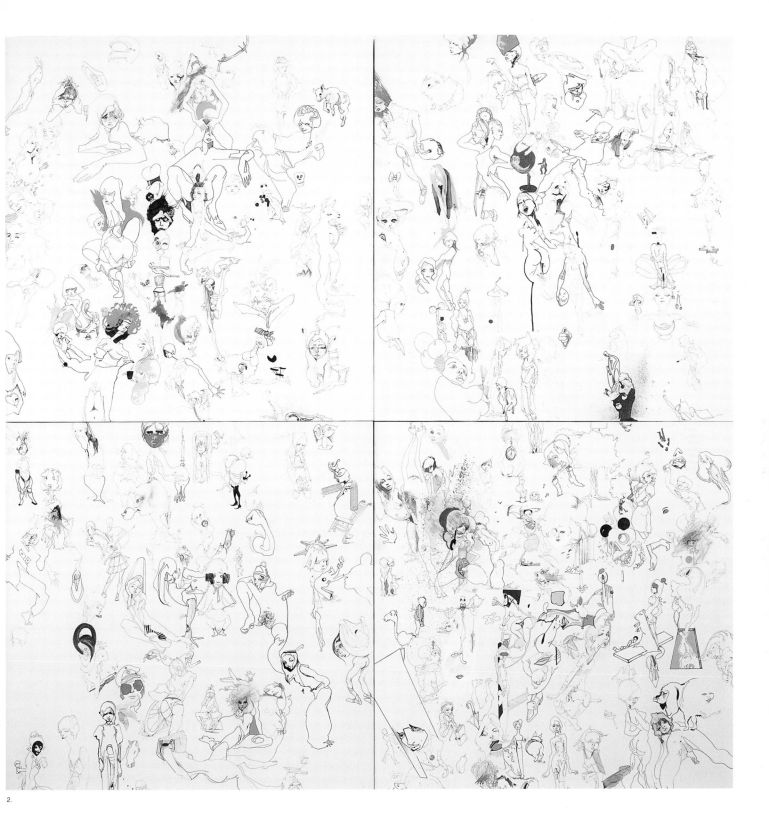

2.

1. <u>UNFORGIVING</u> / Exhibition at Mobile Home Gallery   London 2003   Installation shot
                                                         Photography: Jonnie Bassett

2. <u>FAIR WEATHER FRIENDS</u>   2003   Mixed media on gesso MDF panels 2003
                                                         Photography: Jonnie Bassett

FILTHY LAUGHというタイトルのもと、ファビオによるオリジナルサウンドトラック
が流された。エキシビションは2日間で設置されなければならなかったため、臨機応変
にお互いの意見を取り入れながらインスタレーションを作りこまなければならなかった。

このプロジェクトはユアン・ボリバーによるキュレーションのTRAILERというエキシ
ビションのシリーズで、GUNS'N'ROSESはシリーズ3つ目のエキシビションである。
ロンドン、ブリックレーンのはずれにある未使用の倉庫を利用してジュリーとファビ
オのコラボレーション展が行われた。実際のエキシビションは会場の地下で行われ
FILTHY LAUGHというタイトルのもと、ファビオによるオリジナルサウンドトラック
が流された。エキシビションは2日間で設置されなければならなかったため、臨機応変
にお互いの意見を取り入れながらインスタレーションを作りこまなければならなかった。

This project was curated by Juan Bolivar who was creating a series of independent
exhibitions under the title of Trailer, with Guns 'n' Roses being the third exhibition. The
exhibition was housed in a disused warehouse off Brick Lane, London, with the space
being offered to Julie and Fabio to collaborate in. Their installation was sited in the
basement of the venue and was titled Filthy Laugh with its own soundtrack compiled by
Fabio. The installation is very much site specific with a visceral response to the space.
The exhibition had to be installed within a two-day period so the process of creation and
execution had to be very organic with each protagonist responding to each other's ideas.

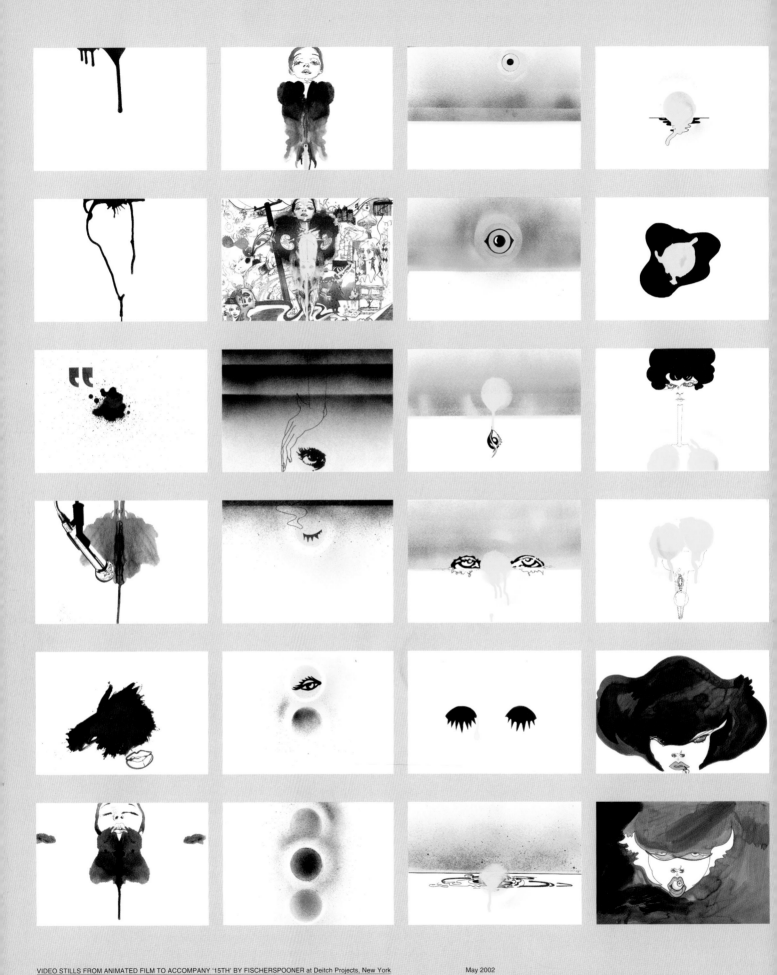

VIDEO STILLS FROM ANIMATED FILM TO ACCOMPANY '15TH' BY FISCHERSPOONER at Deitch Projects, New York   May 2002

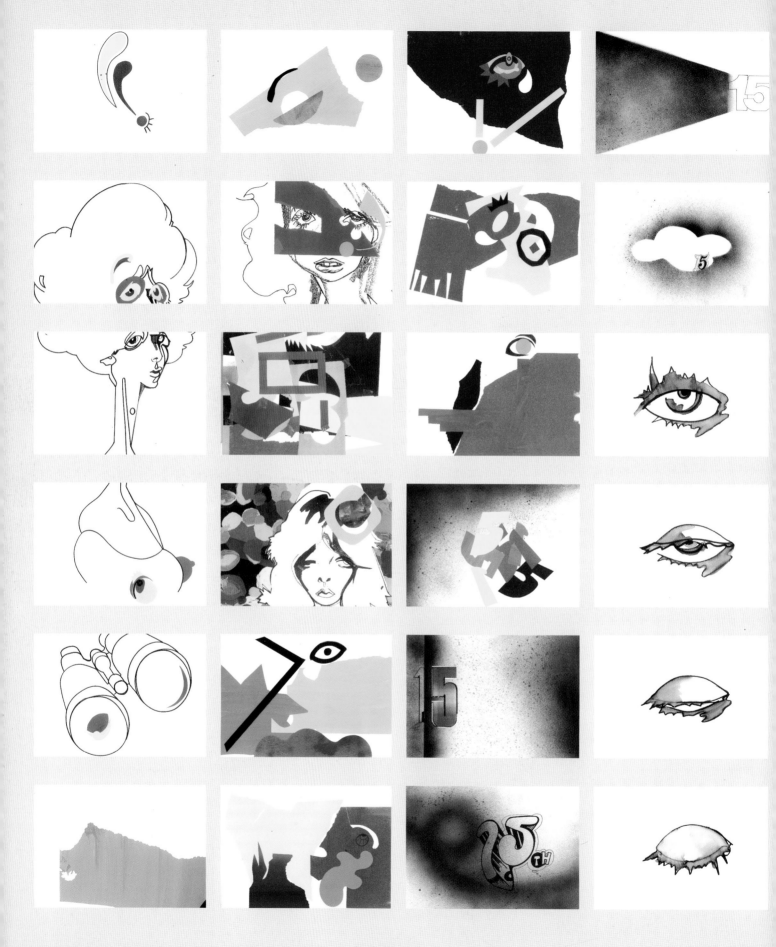

VIDEO STILLS FROM ANIMATED FILM TO ACCOMPANY '15TH' BY FISCHERSPOONER at Deitch Projects, New York   May 2002

1.

1. VIOLENT FEMMES   2002   Paper collage
                                                                         Works from 'Fat-Bottomed Girls'
                                                                         Exhibition at Mobile Home Gallery, London 2002
                                                                         And book of the same name published by TDM Editions 2002

2. ABSTRACT PLAIN   2002   Card, pastel, ink and charcoal

FAT-BOTTOMED GIRLSはモバイルホームギャラリーがまだTHEOBALDS ROADにあった時に開催されたジュリーにとって初の個展である。モバイルホームにてグループ展を行なったことのあったファビオ・アルメイダを通じて当ギャラリーのオーナーであるロニー・シンプソンに出会いジュリーにとってエキサイティングな展開が待っていた。ロニーはジュリーの家で作品を見たことをきっかけに彼女の個展を行なうことにした。個展のねらいはジュリーが子供の頃よく楽しんでいたように、彼女のお気に入りのポップミュージックを絵に描いてもらうことだった。例えばビートルズのSHE'S LEAVING HOMEなどは彼女の特にお気に入りだったらしい。曲名、バンドのスタイル、そして歌詞などが様々な形で絵のモチーフとなった。絵は壁に直接展示されるものもあれば額ぶちに入れられるものもあった。さらには過去の作品に絵を描き足したものなども加えられた。ちょうどほぼ同時期に、彼女のエージェントCLMを通じてフランスのデザイン／出版会社、TDMに出会い個展に関する本を出版することが決まった。個展と同じタイトルの本は半分以上がカタログ的役割を担う出来上がりになった。

This was Julie's first show for the Mobile Home gallery in its former site in Theobalds Road, London. It was exciting time for Julie, having met the owner Ronnie Simpson, through Fabio Almeida, who had been part of a group show at the gallery. Ronnie had seen her wall drawings at their home and offered her a solo show the following year. The intention was for Julie to interpret her favourite pop songs, providing her with the chance to relive a childhood activity of storyboarding songs she liked, She's Leaving Home by The Beatles being fondly remembered. The motivating factors were song title, the attitude of the band and the lyrics, with each song having varying shades of influence. The songs translated themselves onto the walls with some of the work being framed. Julie also found previous work and recycled it by drawing over the top of it. At about the same time an introduction was made to the French designers and publishers, TDM, through her management company CLM, who were keen to create a book of her work. The book of the same title ultimately became a catalogue of the show (or at least half of it).

FAT-BOTTOMED GIRLS AT LARGE / Window installation at Colette   Paris March 2002   Mixed media on paper and emulsion paint

colette

PROJECT 04 MUSIC

MUSIC AND VIDEO

ジュリーはミュージックビデオというメディアに憧れを抱きながらも技術的にはかなり苦手としている。ただこのメディアによりジュリーの作品を新たなフォーマットで見ることができ、また音楽好きのジュリーにとって楽しみを増やしていることは間違いない。シュガーベイブスのNEW YEARのミュージックビデオはファッションページの仕事で写真のコラージュをした後に舞い込んで来た仕事で撮影は2日間に及んだ。1日目はバンドの実写、2日目は他のシーンの撮影に費やされ、撮影されたものにジュリーの絵やスケッチが加えられた。MEL Gのビデオはディレクターがスタイリッシュな内容のミュージックビデオにしたいという要望を実現させるためファッションイラストレーターであるジュリーが起用された。フィッシャースプーナーに関しては、彼らがライブでアーティストの映像を使用しているということを知り実現したものだ。彼らの音楽を聞き、ビジュアル化したい曲を選ぶことができ、ジュリーはWIREというバンドのカバー曲を選択した。実際に作成した映像はニューヨークのダイチプロジェクトやロンドンのロイヤルフェスティバルホールで上映された。プライマル・スクリームとグロスに関してはスリーブのアートワークも作成している。グロスはレコード会社にいろいろと問われることがなく、ジュリーにとってかなり気に入った作品となっている。アルバムの各曲はその歌詞に関連したものが描かれた。イラストレーションの参考になったのは1970年代の女性誌のイラストレーションだった。

SOME VELVET MORNING

プライマル・スクリームはEVIL HEATというアルバムのSOME VELVET MORNINGという曲でナンシー・シナトラとリー・ヘーゼルウッドのデュエットをカバーしている。プライマル・スクリームは非常にはっきりとしたビジュアルスタイルを持っており他を介入させないような強いアイデアを持っている。ケイティー・イングランドの提案によってジュリーがこのプロジェクトに選ばれた。バンドのリードシンガーであるボビー・ギルスピー自身もいろいろとアイデアに溢れており、プロジェクトに好んで関わっていた。彼はビートルズのREVOLVERのカバーや初期のBYRDのアルバムが気に入っており、他にも多数の素材などを持ち寄っていた。またボビーとデュエットをしていたケイト・モスのプライベートポラロイド写真も持っており、それをカバーデザインに使用したいと思っていた。最終的に出来上がったデザインは線描きで歌詞に関係した絵が描かれた。スリーブデザインの制作途中でDAWN SHADFORTH演出のミュージックビデオにもこの絵が使用されることが決まった。

MUSIC AND VIDEO

As a medium Julie is entranced and, at the same time, technically baffled by it. Principally it offers an opportunity to experience Julie's work in a new format and also gives Julie the chance to add to her enjoyment of music. New Year by the Sugababes was commissioned as a result of a fashion editorial piece that had employed a photographic collage execution. The shoot was over two days, one day of live action with the group, the other day shooting different scenarios. These were married with her drawings and sketches and animated. The Mel G video came about following the director requesting more stylised storyboards, an execution that only a fashion illustrator, such as Julie could execute. The Fischerspooner video came about through Julie hearing, through CLM, that they were commissioning individual artists to create moving image to serve as backdrops to their live performances. The brief was to listen to their album and to choose a track to visualise. A cover version of a song by the group Wire was chosen. Julie was invited to New York to see the video in live performance at Deitch Projects. This was followed by another performance at the Royal Festival Hall in London.

Sleeve artwork has covered projects for Primal Scream and Gloss. With Gloss the whole process of sleeve design was approached very openly without any knowledge of the approval processes that record companies employed. Fortunately none of these approvals were needed and the whole project is thought of with great affection by Julie. Every song on the album was accompanied with an illustration referencing the lyrics, the reference point of which were illustrations from women's magazines from the 1970's where the entire story needed to be summed up in one image.

SOME VELVET MORNING

Primal Scream had covered the Nancy Sinatra/Lee Hazelwood duet Some Velvet Morning on their album Evil Heat. Primal Scream has a clearly identifiable visual style that would seem to be impenetrable to any variation. It was Katy England who suggested Julie for the project. Bobby Gillespie, the group's lead singer, also had a great many ideas that he was keen to integrate into the project. He liked the cover of Revolver by the Beatles, early Byrd's album covers along with a plethora of other source material. He also had a pile of informal Polaroid's of Kate Moss (who duets on the cover version of the song with Bobby) and was keen to somehow use them in the artwork. The resulting artwork is linear and flowing on one side referencing the lyrics. The reverse was to be its doppelganger and allude to the darker sexual side of the song. Halfway through creating the sleeve artwork it was decided to use the drawings in the accompanying video, directed by Dawn Shadforth, to be used as a backdrop to the narrative.

Primal Scream and Kate Moss / Some Velvet Morning   November 2003   12" Vinyl label
Design: Intro

COLUMBIA
6744402 6

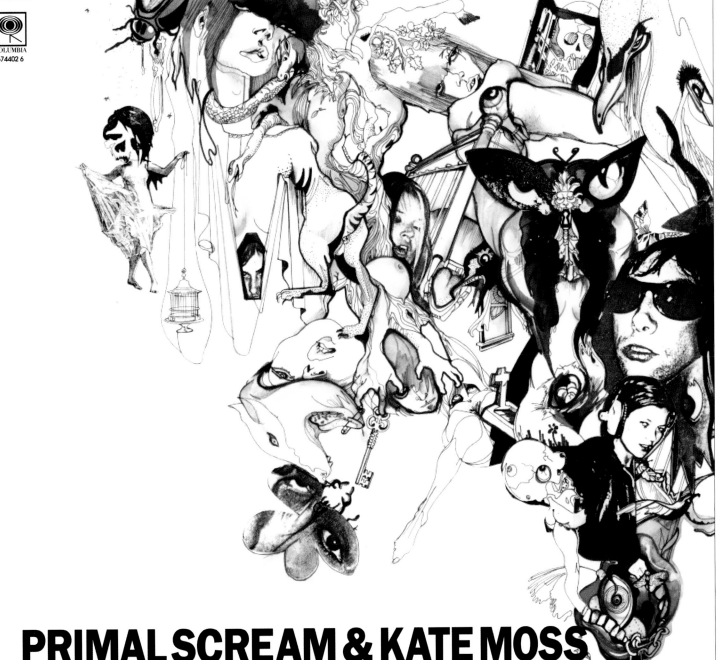

PRIMAL SCREAM & KATE MOSS
SOME VELVET MORNING

Primal Scream and Kate Moss / Some Velvet Morning   November 2003   Single sleeve design (front)
Design: Intro

<u>Primal Scream and Kate Moss / Some Velvet Morning</u>   November 2003   Single sleeve artwork, unpublished.

A1 SOME VELVET
MORNING
Extended mix
B1 COUNTRY
BLUES#1
B2 SOME VELVET
MORNING
Disco Heater Dub

Some Velvet Morning written
by Lee Hazlewood.
Published by Carlin Music Corp.
Country Blues#1 written
by Primal Scream.
Published by Copyright Control.

A1 Co-produced by Andrew Innes &
Jagz Kooner. Mixed by Andrew Innes,
Kevin Shields & Jagz Kooner.
B1 Produced by Andrew Innes
B2 Produced by Two Lone Swordsmen
(Andrew Weatherall & Keith Tenniswood)

Illustration by Julie Verhoeven
Design by Intro

(P) 2003 Sony Music Entertainment
(UK) Ltd.

Distribution by Sony Music
© 2003 Sony Music Entertainment
(UK) Ltd.
Columbia is the exclusive trademark
of Sony Music Entertainment Inc
www.primalscream.net
www.sonymusic.co.uk

674402 6

Thanks to David Holmes.
Dedicated to Rowland S. Howard
& Lydia Lunch.

illustrations by Julie Verhoeven
photographs by Mark Alesky

styling Rachel Ruby Leysol
hair and fur accessories Paul Dixon at Untitled
by The Linen Kensington
make-up Sharon Dowsett
models Jessica at Elite and Kyle

All Tomorrows Parties

VIDEO STILLS FROM POP-PROMO / New Year by Sugababes   Co-directer: Alexander Hemming

GLOSS
NEW
YORK
BOY

GLOSS
MY HEART
BELONGS
TO YOU

GLOSS
THIS IS ALL I NEED

1.

2.

3.

4.

1. <u>MY HEART BELONGS TO YOU</u> BY GLOSS   2000   CD single

2. <u>GLOSS</u> BY GLOSS   2000   CD album

3. <u>NEW YORK BOY</u> BY GLOSS   2000   CD single

4. <u>THIS IS ALL I NEED</u> BY GLOSS   2000   CD single

Entire Gloss campaign: Art direction and design by Blue Source

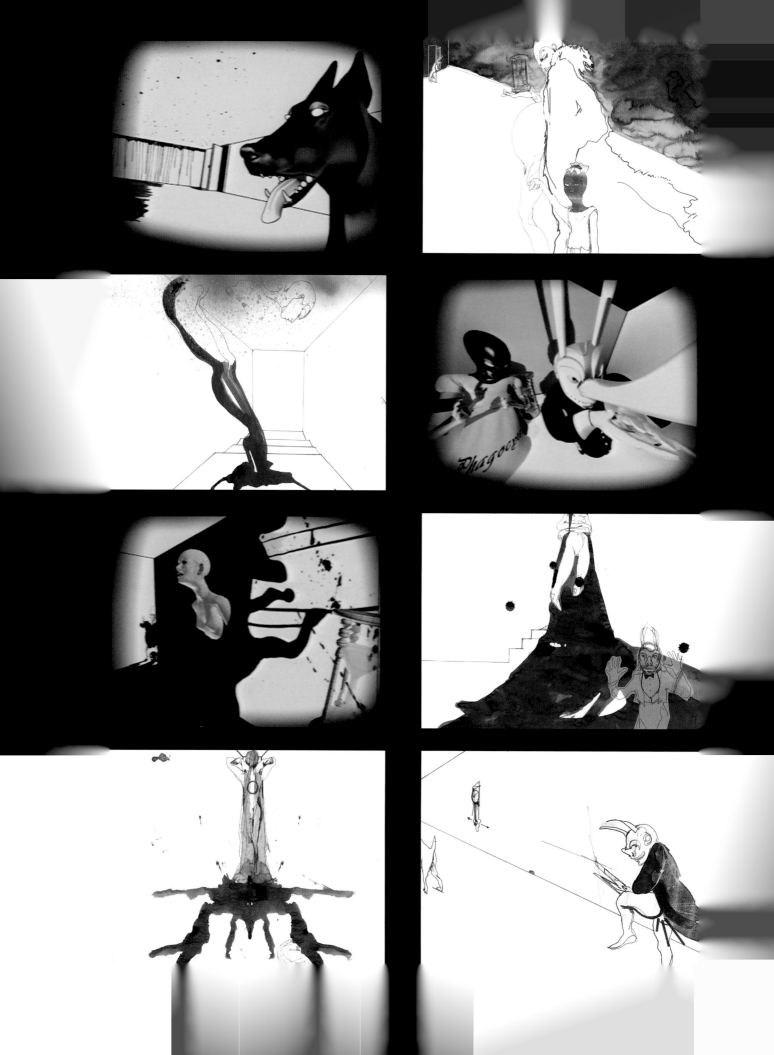

PROJECT 05
EDITORIALS

90年代後半になると、新しいファッションエディターの活躍などで雑誌のエディトリアルでイラストレーションを上手く取り入れることが定着した。この頃はデジタル画像加工や写真等に頼り過ぎることが飽きられてきている時でもあった。

Dazed and Confusedはジュリーの作品を最初に支持しはじめた雑誌のひとつであった。マーク・アレスキーが中心になってジュリーの絵をフォトグラフィーに取り入れる手法を実現させた。この手法はジュリーが特に気に入っているものだ。それからケイティー・イングランドからの依頼でボディーランゲージとジェスチャーをテーマにしたイラストレーションの仕事を受けたり、キャシー・エドワーズの依頼で101足の靴を特集したページを担当したりもした。これらはかなりの成功を収め、その後にもビューティー特集やマネキンをペイントしたページなどの仕事もこなした。この仕事は作品の領域を3次元に広げた。それほどたたないうちにSELF SERVICEやTHE FACEなどもすぐに彼女に仕事の依頼をし始めた。

これらの仕事に関しては、締めきりという概念を抜かせばジュリーが非常に楽しんで取り組むもののひとつだといえる。彼女にとって理想的なのは一回だけ打ち合わせをし、それをもとに作品を作り上げることだ。あまり打ち合わせをしすぎると、そのプロジェクトの統一感を失うことにつながると考えているからだ。それぞれのプロジェクトはその性質が異なるが彼女の仕事に対する手法は常に変わらずに様々な仕事に取り込んでいる。数年前には数ページだったものが今では大々的にファッションストーリーなどを担当するまでになった。

As the 1990's drew to a close, the concept of utilising illustration as part of magazine editorials became a more comfortable notion, particularly with a new breed of fashion editors and the greater preponderance of titles. This was also tied in with a thirst to see something new that did not rely on digital trickery or a complete reliance on reality. Dazed and Confused magazine were one of the first magazines to champion her work, with Mark Alesky being key to allowing this to happen, with elements of her drawing being introduced onto photographic images. This is a method of execution that Julie is particularly fond of. Katy England commissioned a project around the themes of body language and gestures with Cathy Edwards commissioning a shoe feature entitled 101 Shoes. The project was very successful with a beauty feature following soon after that featured painted mannequins. This allowed Julie to develop her drawings into a more three dimensional form. Self Service and The Face magazines were quick to follow this lead.

It is identified as one of the most enjoyable areas that Julie works in, despite the deadlines. In an ideal world the brief is just one conversation and that work evolves from this exchange. If there is too much conversation then the commission loses its own internal momentum. With each commission the style varies slightly (this is the nature of the work) but the working method remains constant with the work being completed by hand to a much larger scale than the magazine page. What started out as a couple of pages have now become whole stories.

DAZED

pretty vacant

PHOTOGRAPHY **JENNY VAN SOMMERS**
SPRING AND MAKE UP **JULIE VERHOEVEN** **84**
DECEMBER 2001 UK £3.20 US $8.25

**46 pages of
anti-beauty**

**selma blair
john maeda
homegrown music for 2002**

A PROPOS 3/6
HELMUT LANG SPRING/SUMMER 2001
ILLUSTRATION BY JULIE VERHOEVEN

1.

2.

1. APROPOS / Published in Self Service   Spring / Summer 2001

2. 101 SHOES / Published in Dazed and Confused   October 2000

1.

2.

CREATED RELEVANCE

A shock to the system has launched many creative people on an evaluation of the broader significance of what we do. What is the purpose of art? How well do we understand, and are we understood by, the cultures around us? What is the effect of our efforts? A forum of thinkers provides their statements on social consciousness and artistic expression. **Illustration by Julie Verhoeven**

1.

Julie's jewel box safari

2.

3.

4.

please turn over →

PROJECT 06
LOUIS VUITTON

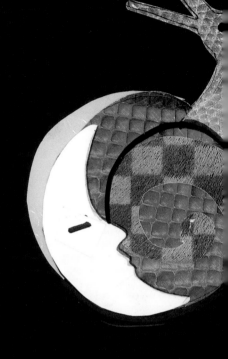

ちょうどジュリーがエディトリアルの仕事を集中的にこなしていた時に、彼女の作品がルイ・ヴィトンのファッションディレクター、マーク・ジェイコブスの目にとまり仕事が舞い込んできた。NYのファッションデザイナーSTEPHEN SPROUSEを起用して成功を収めていたマークは、ぜひ次のラインにジュリーを加えたいと意欲に燃えていた。アイデアや画像がメールを通じてひっきりなしに取り交わされ最終的にルイ・ヴィトンの伝統的なモノグラムに施されるコラージュへと発展していった。マーク自身のアイデアは固まっており、それを実現させるのはジュリーの手にかかっていた。あるバッグには黄昏を思わせる絵が施され他のバッグには妖精物語を表すものなどが作られた。

作業としてはじめに線描きがベースとなった。全てのレザーはカラーコピーされコラージュが上手く作成できるように配慮された。最終的に作られたコラージュはそのままバッグに反映され妥協なしに製造が進められていった。この頃にマークはキティーちゃんのようにキャラクターのバッグや大きな財布などを作れないかと考えていた。このプロジェクトはジュリーによってスタイルやアイデアの移行ではなく彼女のクリエイティブ作業に新たな一面を加えたといえる。

The Louis Vuitton project came about during an intense period of editorial commissions that had attracted the attention of Louis Vuitton's fashion director Marc Jacobs. Having had success with a previous range designed by the New York fashion designer Stephen Sprouse, he had had some ideas for another range and was keen to involve Julie in the project. A series of ideas and images were mailed which were further refined into creating a collage effect of all the classic Vuitton monogrammed leathers. Marc was very clear in his ideas and it was up to Julie to supply the artwork to realise the concept. One bag was to evoke twilight, for example, whilst another was to allude to fairy tales.

The process began with line drawings as a foundation. Resorting to colour photocopying all the leathers that were available so the collage technique could be better employed. The resulting paper collage could be directly translated, without compromise, into the production process bearing in mind that it was necessary to use as many of the monograms, colours and embossings. From this point Marc had the idea of developing a range of small character bags or giant purses using an abstracted notion of the Hello Kitty range of accessories. The project does not represent a departure in the style, ideas or execution of Julie's work but serves to add another facet to her creative processes.

1.   REVERSE OF 'TWILIGHT' BAG / Collage Artwork

2.   'TORTOISE' DESIGN IN REAL / From Louis Vuitton catwalk show   Spring / Summer 2002

3.   FRONT OF 'TWILIGHT' BAG / Collage Artwork   Design for Louis Vuitton   Spring / Summer 2002

1.

2.

3.

4.

PAGE **61 AND 62** JULIE VERHOEVEN PROJECT 06 LOUIS VUITTON

1. <u>REVERSE OF 'SNAIL' DESIGN BAG</u> / Collage artworks   Spring / Summer 2002

2. <u>REVERSE OF 'TORTOISE' DESIGN BAG</u> / Collage artworks   Spring / Summer 2002

3. <u>FRONT OF 'SNAIL' DESIGN BAG</u> / Collage artworks   Spring / Summer 2002

4. <u>FRONT OF 'TORTOISE' DESIGN BAG</u> / Collage artworks   Spring / Summer 2002

Prêt-à-Porter, Calzature, Pelletteria. In vendita unicamente nei negozi esclusivi Louis Vuitton. Tel. 800 30 89 80   www.vuitton.com

LOUIS VUITTON

Ready-to-wear, Shoes, Leather Goods. Sold exclusively in Louis Vuitton stores. Tel. 020 7399 4050 www.vuitton.com

LOUIS VUITTON

1.

2.

3.

1. 'FAT FROG' Mini-bag / LOUIS VUITTON ADVERTISING   Spring / Summer 2002   Photography: Mert Alas and Marcus Piggott

2. 'SNAIL' Bag / LOUIS VUITTON ADVERTISING   Spring / Summer 2002   Photography: Mert Alas and Marcus Piggott

3. FRONT OF 'GIRAFFE' / Design bag Collage Artwork   Spring / Summer 2002

ANSWERS

JULIE VERHOEVEN

ROAD LONDON SE~~~~~ UK

T. 020 7~~~~~ F. 020 7~~~~~ E. JULIE~~~~~~~~~~~~~~~~~

1. When do you most feel the presence of "design" around you?

SHOPPING

2. What is your favourite shape?

AN EXCLAIMATION MARK

3. What was your happiest moment in your work experience?

STILL WAITING

4. Please list your 3 favourite colours.

LAWN GREEN · CERISE · JADE

5. What do you hate the most?

ILL HEALTH and MY ACNE

6. Please list up your 3 favourites materials.

PILOT PEN · LEADPENCIL · TAFFETTA

7. Where is your most favourite place?

IN BED

8. Please list up your 3 favourite designers.

FOREVER CHANGING

9. Please define the word "design".

DIFFICULT

10. Please list up your 3 favourite words.

HOOT · HIDEOUS · NONSENSE

*late additions!
...also despicable, deceitful low-life including
step mother-from-hell; Ann Monk/Theobald/Hopkins/Verhoeven!
Plus the witch who stole Howards drawings
and not forgetting, callous Tine, of course!*

EDITORIAL
CREDIT

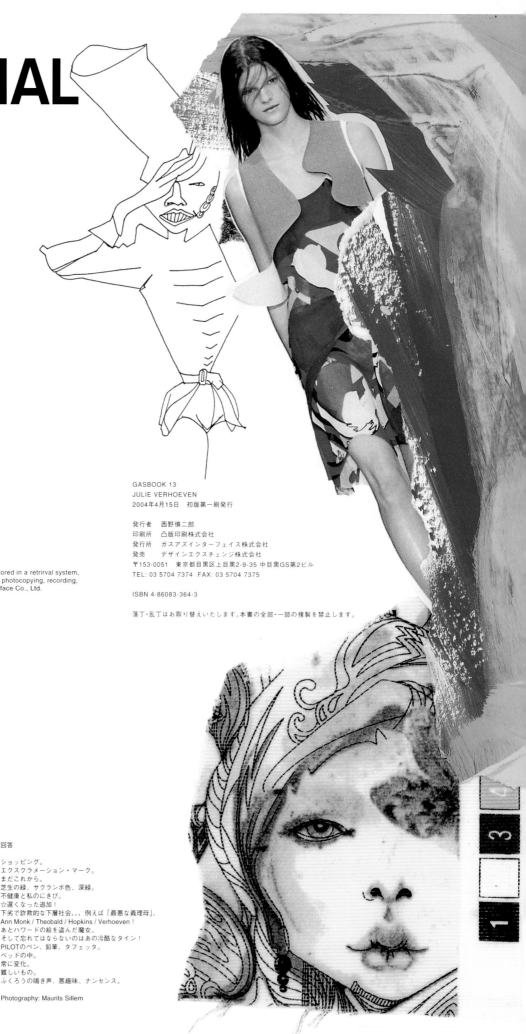

GASBOOK 13
JULIE VERHOEVEN

COVER ART WORK: Julie Verhoeven

EDITORIAL DIRECTOR: Toru Hachiga
TEXT: Daniel Mason

STUDIO PHOTO: Maurits Sillem

DESIGN: Ai Fukasawa, Fabio Almeida
FORMAT DESIGN: Hideki Inaba

COORDINATION/TRANSLATION: Ayako Terashima

PUBLISHER: Shinjiro Nishino

Published in Japan in 2004
Gas As Interface Co., Ltd.
Nakameguro GS Dai2 Bldg 2-9-35 Kamimeguro
Meguro-ku Tokyo 153-0051 Japan
Phone: 81 3 5704 7374 Fax: 81 3 5704 7375
e-mail: info@gasasif.com
http://www.gasasif.com

ISBN 4-86083-364-3

Printed in Japan by Toppan Printing Co.,Ltd.

First Printing, 2004

GASBOOK 13
JULIE VERHOEVEN
2004年4月15日　初版第一刷発行

発行者　西野慎二郎
印刷所　凸版印刷株式会社
発行所　ガスアズインターフェイス株式会社
発売　　デザインエクスチェンジ株式会社
〒153-0051　東京都目黒区上目黒2-9-35 中目黒GS第2ビル
TEL: 03 5704 7374　FAX: 03 5704 7375

ISBN 4-86083-364-3

PAGE **62 AND 63**

質問

01) 身の周りで最もデザインを感じる時は？
02) 好きなフォルムは？
03) これまで制作活動を続けてきて一番うれしかったことは？
04) 好きなカラーを順番に３つ並べて下さい。
05) 嫌いな事は？

06) 好きなマテリアルを３つ答えて下さい。
07) あなたが一番好きな場所は？
08) 好きなデザイナーを３人あげてください。
09) あなたにとってデザインとは？
10) 好きな言葉を３つ教えて下さい。

STUDIO

回答

ショッピング。
エクスクラメーション・マーク。
まだこれから。
芝生の緑、サクランボ色、深緑。
不健康と私のにきび。
☆遅くなった追加！
下劣で詐欺的な下層社会... 例えば「最悪な義理母」、
Ann Monk / Theobald / Hopkins / Verhoeven！
あとハワードの絵を盗んだ魔女。
そして忘れてはならないのはあの冷酷なタイン！
PILOTのペン、鉛筆、タフェッタ。
ベッドの中。
常に変化。
難しいもの。
ふくろうの鳴き声、悪趣味、ナンセンス。

Photography: Maurits Sillem